D1765750

BEGINNING WITH JOHN'S GOSPEL

The Introduction to John's Gospel simply explained

Susan Harding

Illustrated by
Helen A Noyce

THE BANNER OF TRUTH TRUST

THE BANNER OF TRUTH TRUST

3 Murrayfield Road, Edinburgh EH12 6EL
P.O. Box 621, Carlisle, Pennsylvania 17013, USA

*

© The Banner of Truth 1996
First published 1996
ISBN 0 85151 687 4

*

Scripture quotations are taken from
the New King James Version
© 1982 by Thomas Nelson, Inc.

Printed and bound in Singapore
by SNP Printing Pte Ltd

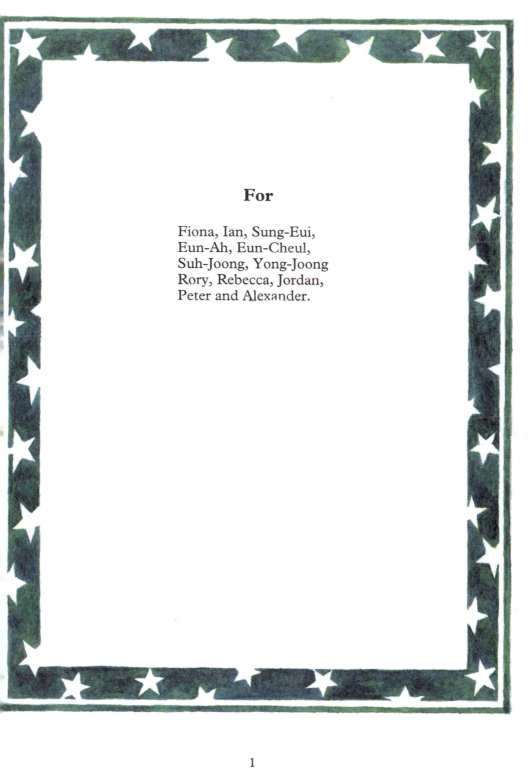

For

Fiona, Ian, Sung-Eui,
Eun-Ah, Eun-Cheul,
Suh-Joong, Yong-Joong
Rory, Rebecca, Jordan,
Peter and Alexander.

Introduction

There was a time when people thought there was something magic about the part of John's Gospel which we are going to look at. This was because the words seemed difficult and mysterious to them.

But when the apostle John wrote his book, he explained why he did so: That you may believe that Jesus is the Christ, the Son of God, and that believing, you may have life in his name. John wanted people to understand clearly what he wrote, so that they should believe. We are going to look at the first eighteen verses of John's Gospel — often called the Prologue — to see what he is teaching us. These verses are really an introduction to the rest of the Gospel. So we will also read small sections from the main part of John's book, which link in with the teaching of the Prologue, or introduction. You may like to read the Prologue verses in the morning, and the study passages in the evening.

1st

Night

John the Writer

John — who wrote this book — was one of the twelve apostles whom Jesus chose to be witnesses of his life and work. He went about with Jesus from the beginning of his work as a preacher and a worker of miracles. But he also saw Jesus being crucified, and was a witness of his resurrection when he came back from the dead.

John and his brother James were fishermen. They worked as partners with their father Zebedee. But when Jesus called them, they left their business and followed him. With Peter they were the apostles who were closest to Jesus: he took these three to be with him when he was transfigured, and when he prayed before his death, in the garden of Gethsemane.

John, in his account of Jesus' life, speaks of himself as 'the disciple whom Jesus loved', rather than using his own name.

We know that John lived to an old age. He wrote three letters to the New Testament church, as well as this Gospel and the Book of Revelation. Probably John wrote his Gospel after Matthew, Mark and Luke had written their accounts of Jesus' life. John seems to assume that his readers will already know the things about Jesus which these other Gospels tell us.

John's Gospel, like the other books in the New Testament, is written in Greek.

In the beginning was the Word, and the Word was with God, and the Word was God.

John, the writer, describes the person he is going to write about: a person he has known very well.

What would you say about a close friend, if you were starting to write a book about him or her?

His name, and perhaps his parents' names

> Where he was born

> What he looks like

> What sort of person he is.

John could have written down all these things about Jesus – he was a real human being, as we are. But instead, John chose to describe the same person in this way:

> In the beginning was the Word

> And the Word was with God

> And the Word was God.

From this we can see that John wants us to understand that Jesus, whom he calls 'the Word' is GOD! No other human being could be described in this way. It is a description of God.

Study passage.

At the end of his book, John tells his readers how one of Jesus' other apostles, Thomas, comes to realise that Jesus is God. It happens after Jesus had come back to life, and shown himself to his disciples.

But Thomas, called Didymus, one of the twelve, was not with them when Jesus came. The other disciples therefore said to him, 'We have seen the Lord'. But he said to them, 'Unless I see in his hands the print of the nails, and put my finger into the print of the nails, and put my hand into his side, I will not believe'. And after eight days his disciples were again inside, and Thomas with them. Jesus came, the doors being shut, and stood in the midst, and said, 'Peace to you!'

Then he said to Thomas, 'Reach your finger here, and look at my hands; and reach your hand here, and put it into my side. Do not be unbelieving, but believing.'

And Thomas answered and said to him, 'My Lord and my God!'

John 20, vv.24–29

7

The Word

What is the name of your teacher? Do you ever say, 'Teacher says we must do this'? If you do, you are giving your teacher another name, a title. You are calling him or her 'teacher' — because of course, he or she teaches you.

We have already noticed that John does not give Jesus his ordinary human name at the beginning of this story. He gives him another name, or title, which explains what Jesus does for us. He calls him, 'the Word'.

Human beings use words. Animals and plants do not talk to each other. They do not use words. But human beings do because God has taught them to do so.

One of the first things a mother does to her new baby is to talk to him or her. When she talks, she uses words. And soon the baby learns to say words too. That is how the baby learns to think and to know about everything. And that is how the baby gets to know his mother. Once we start to talk to people we get to know them.

We talk — we use words — because we have been made by God to copy him in this way. God is *the Word*. God the Father and God the Son speak to each other.

When John says: **'In the beginning was the Word'**, he is teaching us something very important. God uses words: he talks to us. How does he do that? Well, John says, Jesus is the Word. He is God, talking to us.

Study passage

In this passage, Jesus himself tells us how important his words are. If we love Jesus, we will keep his words, and God will make his home with us. Notice how God the Father, the Son and the Holy Spirit, all bring the word of God to us. The Holy Spirit reminded John of all the things Jesus said, so that he would be able to write them down in this book.

Jesus... said... 'If anyone loves me, he will keep my word; and my Father will love him, and we will come to him and make our home with him. He who does not love me does not keep my words; and the word which you hear is not mine but the Father's who sent me. These things I have spoken to you while being present with you. But the Helper, the Holy Spirit, whom the Father will send in my name, he will teach you all things, and bring to your remembrance all things that I said to you.'

John 14, vv. 23–26

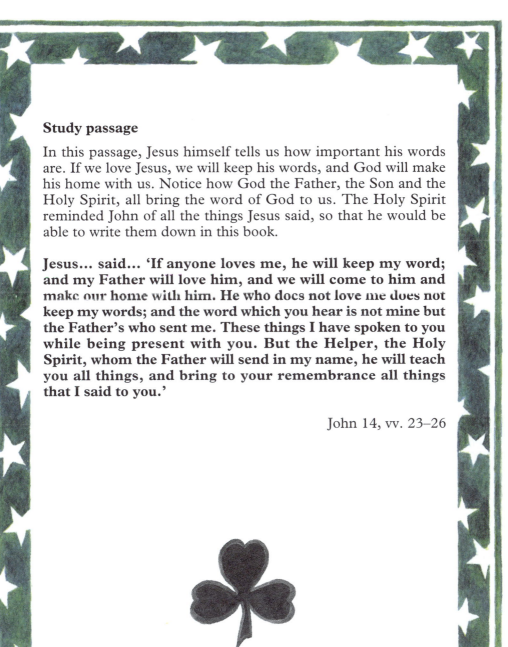

In the beginning was the Word

Now John tells us something else in the first verse of his book, which is even harder to understand. He tells us that Jesus was alive right in the beginning: 'In the beginning was the Word.'

We cannot say that about any other person. All human beings are born in time, after the world was made. But Jesus was there before that time.

Then John says that Jesus, the Word, was with God. From this, we think of how there must have been two persons: Jesus, and God. But John says something more. He says, 'the Word was God' There are two persons, Jesus and God. But Jesus, the Word, is God as well:

The Word was God.

He was in the beginning with God.

In other parts of the Bible we learn that God is three persons, and yet one God: God the Father, God the Son and God the Holy Spirit.

Study passage.

Here Jesus angers and amazes his listeners by telling them that he was alive before Abraham — who had lived many hundreds of years before. He says that 'Before Abraham was, I am'. 'I AM' (Jehovah) was the name God used in the Old Testament, to describe the fact that he had always existed. When John writes that 'in the beginning was the Word', he is teaching us the same thing about Jesus: he had always existed.

(Jesus said) 'Most assuredly, I say to you, if anyone keeps my word he shall never see death'.

Then the Jews said to him, 'Now we know that you have a demon! Abraham is dead, and the prophets; and you say, "If anyone keeps my word he shall never taste death". Are you greater than our father Abraham, who is dead? And the prophets are dead. Whom do you make yourself out to be?'

Jesus answered, 'If I honour myself, my honour is nothing. It is my Father who honours me, of whom you say that he is your God. Yet you have not known him, but I know him. And if I say, "I do not know him", I shall be a liar like you; but I do know him and keep his word.

Your father Abraham rejoiced to see my day, and he saw it and was glad.'

Then the Jews said to him, 'You are not yet fifty years old, and have you seen Abraham?'
Jesus said to them, 'Most assuredly, I say to you, before Abraham was, I AM.'

John 8, vv.51–58

11

**All things were made through him,
and without him nothing was made that
was made.**

John is still talking about his friend Jesus, the man he often had
dinner with, and went around with. Yet this man, he says, is God.
He gives him this special other name — this title — the Word:
God talking to us.

Now, in verse three he adds that not only was his friend before
time began — in the beginning — but he also made everything!

Imagine drawing a very large circle. Then imagine you could put
everything into it that the Word made: everything there is!

Now imagine drawing another circle. This time, leave it empty.
That set contains the things which were made without the Word.
This empty set shows us that nothing was made without the
Word.

Study passage.

John in this part of his book, describes the first miracle which Jesus did. It showed that he had power over the things he had created – to change water into wine. In the beginning he had made all things out of nothing: the work of creation. Now, in time, this miracle showed that he had power to make things new: that is the work of salvation. Jesus' miracles were always done to help people. But they were also signs of his power, as God, to save them. In this example, to change them from being one thing – sinners – into something else – his saints.

On the third day there was a wedding in Cana of Galilee, and the mother of Jesus was there.
Now both Jesus and his disciples were invited to the wedding. And when they ran out of wine, the mother of Jesus said to him, 'They have no wine' Jesus said to her, 'Woman, what does your concern have to do with me? My hour has not yet come'.
His mother said to the servants, 'Whatever he says to you, do it.'
Now there were set there six waterpots of stone...
Jesus said to them, 'Fill the waterpots with water.' And they filled them to the brim. And he said to them, 'Draw some out now, and take it to the master of the feast.' And they took it. When the master of the feast had tasted the water that was made wine, and did not know where it came from, (but the servants who had drawn the water knew), the master of the feast called the bridegroom. And he said to him, 'Every man at the beginning sets out the good wine, and when the guests have well drunk, then that which is inferior; but you have kept the good wine until now'.

John 2, vv.1–11

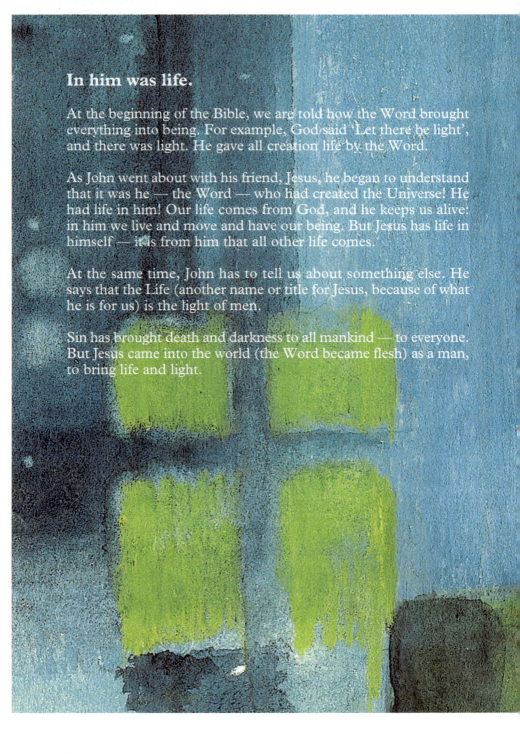

In him was life.

At the beginning of the Bible, we are told how the Word brought everything into being. For example, God said 'Let there be light', and there was light. He gave all creation life by the Word.

As John went about with his friend, Jesus, he began to understand that it was he — the Word — who had created the Universe! He had life in him! Our life comes from God, and he keeps us alive: in him we live and move and have our being. But Jesus has life in himself — it is from him that all other life comes.

At the same time, John has to tell us about something else. He says that the Life (another name or title for Jesus, because of what he is for us) is the light of men.

Sin has brought death and darkness to all mankind — to everyone. But Jesus came into the world (the Word became flesh) as a man, to bring life and light.

Study passage

Here is an account of another of Jesus' miracles. Again, it is a sign as well as a kind deed. Jesus brings his friend Lazarus, who had been dead for some days, back to life. He shows that he is the one who gives life to the dead. This life is eternal. It is the life which is in himself: through him our sins are taken away and so we are brought back to God again.

Then Jesus, again groaning in himself, came to the tomb. It was a cave, and a stone lay against it. Jesus said, 'Take away the stone'.

Martha, the sister of him who was dead, said to him, 'Lord, by this time there is a stench, for he has been dead four days.' Jesus said to her, 'Did I not say to you that if you would believe you would see the glory of God?'

Then they took away the stone from the place where the dead man was lying... Jesus cried with a loud voice, 'Lazarus, come forth!' And he who had died came out bound hand and foot with graveclothes, and his face was wrapped with a cloth. Jesus said to them, 'Loose him, and let him go.'

John 11, vv.38–41

The life was the light of men.

Have you heard people say that they are in the dark about something? They mean that they do not know about that thing. Most of all, people are in the dark about God. They do not know who he is. They certainly do not know him as a person.

Being in the dark about God is what death really is. It means people are separated from God, who is real life. In one sense they are living — they are walking about and so on — but in another sense they are dead, because they are cut off from the living God, and are in darkness.

To people like this, Jesus comes: the life was the light of men. To people who are in the dark about God, he shows them God and so brings them life.

Study passage

Here Jesus speaks about the power which only he has, to give life to people — people who are 'dead' because they are cut off from the living God. Hearing Jesus' word is what brings them back to life. When Jesus brought Lazarus back to life by his word: 'Lazarus, come forth', this was a picture in action of what he does to people who are dead in sin.

Most assuredly, I say to you, he who hears my word and believes in him who sent me has everlasting life, and shall not come into judgement, but has passed from death into life.
Most assuredly, I say to you, the hour is coming, and now is, when the dead will hear the voice of the Son of God; and those who hear will live. For as the Father has life in himself, so he has granted the Son to have life in himself, and has given him authority to execute judgement also, because he is the Son of Man.

John 5, vv.24–27

And the light shines in the darkness, and the darkness did not comprehend it.

Imagine a room in complete darkness. Now switch on the light.

The light shines in the darkness.

People are in darkness: they cannot see the truth: they cannot understand about God. But Jesus, the light, shines into that darkness.

We are told here that our minds are the exact opposite of what God is. They are darkness, and he is light. The good news is, that in Jesus, God has switched on the light.

But still, the darkness itself does not understand this. All through his book about Jesus, John has to tell us about people who were against him, and who chose to stay in the dark.

Study passage

The first verse here explains the cost to God of sending light into the world: the giving of his only Son. We may be so used to this idea that we take it for granted. But we should be amazed. Then John explains more about people's reaction to the light God sends. People do not come to the light, because it shows up the badness of what they do.

For God so loved the world, that he gave his only begotten Son, that whoever believes in him should not perish but have everlasting life. For God did not send his Son into the world to condemn the world, but that the world through him might be saved.

He who believes in him is not condemned; but he who does not believe is condemned already, because he has not believed in the name of the only begotten Son of God. And this is the condemnation, that the light has come into the world, and men loved darkness rather than light, because their deeds were evil. For everyone practising evil hates the light and does not come to the light, lest his deeds should be exposed.

But he who does the truth comes to the light, that his deeds may be clearly seen, that they have been done in God.

John 3, vv.16–21

There was a man sent from God whose name was John. This man came for a witness, to bear witness of the Light, that all through him might believe.

Up until now John the writer has been talking about his friend, the man called Jesus. But we have seen that John does not talk about him as a man — although he was one. He describes him as the eternal God, the Word, the Light, as Life itself.

But now he stops for a moment to talk about a man who was, like us, just a man — a man whose name, like the writer's, was John. So we have John the writer, and now, John the Baptist.

Unlike Jesus, this John was just an ordinary human being — just a man. But he was special in one way — he was sent from God.

We can think of John the Baptist as being a bit like a postman.

When the postman comes, we hardly notice him. We are only interested in the letter he brings us, from someone we love. We tear it open, and read the message. And the postman goes away unnoticed.

John the Baptist was sent by God with a message. But people are not interested in God. So John has, as it were, to open the letter and read it to them, to make them listen.

People are in the dark, so John is sent to point them to the light. John brings the message, like the postman. But his message is from God, and it says: look at the light. That is the message which leads men to faith.

Study passage

Here is an example of John the Baptist pointing people to Jesus — or bearing witness to the light. Notice how God the Father has told John how he will recognise God the Son: God the Holy Spirit will come down on him like a dove, and will stay on him. So John the Baptist is a witness that Jesus is the Son of God.

The next day John saw Jesus coming towards him, and said, 'Behold! The Lamb of God who takes away the sin of the world!

This is he of whom I said, "After me comes a man who is preferred before me, for he was before me". I did not know him; but that he should be revealed to Israel, therefore I came baptizing with water.'

And John bore witness, saying 'I saw the Spirit descending from heaven like a dove, and he remained upon him. I did not know him, but he who sent me to baptize with water said to me, "Upon whom you see the spirit descending, and remaining on him, this is he who baptizes with the Holy Spirit."

And I have seen and testified that this is the son of God'.

John 1, vv.29–34

He was not that Light, but was sent to bear witness of that Light

Already John the writer has made us notice that John the Baptist was only a man. But because he was sent from God — and so was special — some people thought that John himself was the Light.

Because people are in the dark, they often put special men in the place of God. They did this with John. They were more interested in the postman than in the message and its sender.

John the writer wanted his readers to know that this was wrong: John the Baptist was only the person who pointed to the Light in the darkness — like the look-out on a ship, shouting out when he spots the light-house in the night.

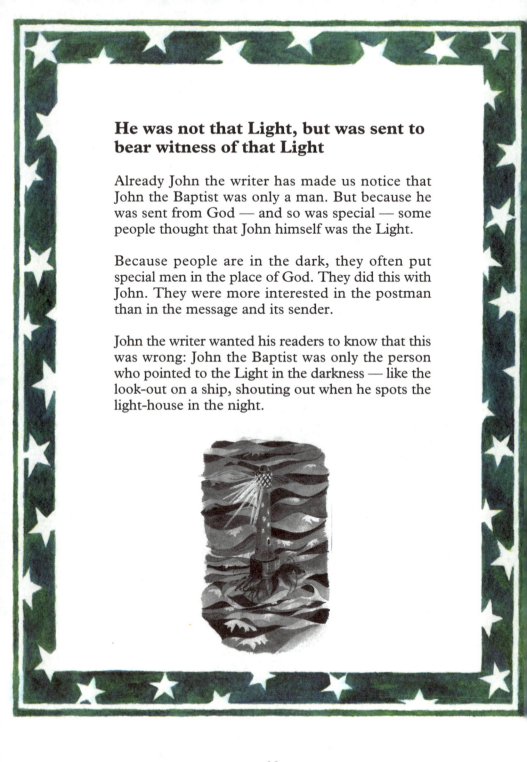

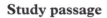

Study passage

When people came to ask John who he was, John the Baptist described himself as just a voice! We can see from this how anxious he was that people should not be making a fuss of him. They should just be listening to his voice: the message: 'Make straight the way of the Lord.'

Now this is the testimony of John, when the Jews sent priests and Levites from Jerusalem to ask him, 'Who are you?' he confessed and did not deny, but confessed, 'I am not the Christ'. And they asked him, 'What then? Are you Elijah?' He said, 'I am not'. 'Are you the Prophet?' And he answered, 'No'.

Then they said to him, 'Who are you, that we may give an answer to those who sent us? What do you say about yourself?' He said, 'I am

"The voice of one crying in the wilderness: Make straight the way of the Lord",

as the prophet Isaiah said.'

John 1, vv.19–23

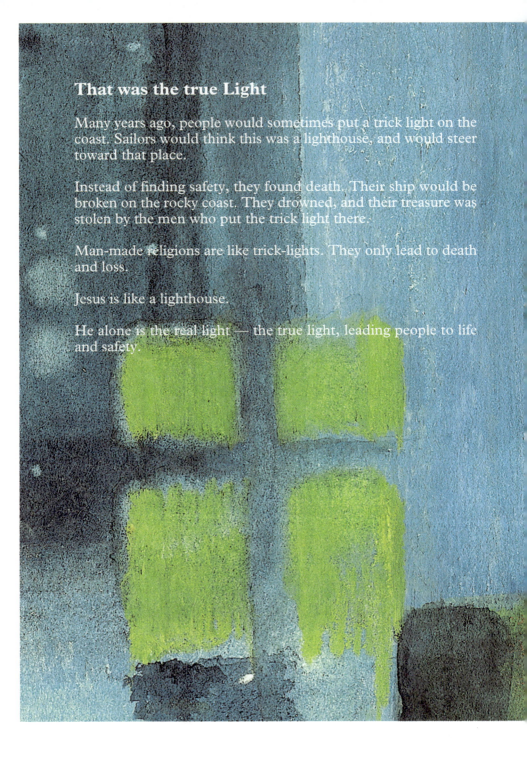

That was the true Light

Many years ago, people would sometimes put a trick light on the coast. Sailors would think this was a lighthouse, and would steer toward that place.

Instead of finding safety, they found death. Their ship would be broken on the rocky coast. They drowned, and their treasure was stolen by the men who put the trick light there.

Man-made religions are like trick-lights. They only lead to death and loss.

Jesus is like a lighthouse.

He alone is the real light — the true light, leading people to life and safety.

Study passage

Jesus describes the people who follow him as being like sheep hearing the shepherd's voice. He himself is the good shepherd, who owns the sheep and really loves them. Sometimes the shepherd sleeps in the gap in the sheepfold, and so in this way he is the door too. Jesus says that fake religious teachers are like thieves and strangers. A hireling is a man who doesn't own the sheep and doesn't care about them: he is there only for the sake of the money he will earn.

Then Jesus said to them again, 'Most assuredly, I say to you, I am the door of the sheep. All who ever came before me are thieves and robbers, but the sheep did not hear them.

I am the door. If anyone enters by me, he will be saved, and will go in and out and find pasture. The thief does not come except to steal, and to kill, and to destroy. I have come that they may have life, and that they may have it more abundantly.

I am the good shepherd. The good shepherd gives his life for the sheep. But he who is a hireling and not the shepherd, one who does not own the sheep, sees the wolf coming and leaves the sheep and flees; and the wolf catches the sheep and scatters them. The hireling flees because he is a hireling and does not care about the sheep.
I am the good shepherd; and I know my sheep, and am known by my own.'

John 10, vv.7–14

25

Which gives light to every man

This world is a place of darkness — the darkness which is in people's souls — the darkness of sin.

It is a place completely alien to God. There is no light coming from this world. Any light that comes must come from God himself. It must come *into* the world.

Any person who has any light, has it from the true light which comes from God: from Jesus.

Imagine you have a box of old candles. They have no light of their own. You must have a match to light them with. Not one single person has light, unless it first comes from Jesus.

He is the light that comes into the world, which gives light to each person.

Study passage

Jesus' miracles were always signs, or pictures in action, of what he does for people's souls. Here, he has made a man born blind, able to see. He uses it as a picture of the blindness, or darkness, which everybody has if they do not believe in him. The people who were against Jesus — the Pharisees — believed they had light in themselves. They said: 'We see'. Jesus points out that their sin therefore stayed with them. They did not believe in him. People who admit they are blind (that is, sinful) receive their sight from Jesus — who gives light to every man.

Jesus said to the man he had healed of blindness: 'Do you believe in the Son of God?'
He answered and said, 'Who is he, Lord, that I may believe in him?'

And Jesus said to him, 'You have both seen him and it is he who is talking with you. Then he said, 'Lord, I believe!' And he worshipped him.
And Jesus said, 'For judgment I have come into this world, that those who do not see may see, and that those who see may be made blind.'
Then some of the Pharisees who were with him heard these words, and said to him, 'Are we blind also?'
Jesus said to them, 'If you were blind, you would have no sin; but now you say, 'We see'. Therefore your sin remains.'

John 9, vv.35–41

He was in the world, and the world was made through him, and the world did not know him.

John says something now which should make us very upset. But because we are affected by sin, we hardly notice what he says. Think of how a horse knows its own master. Think of how a small child knows its own parents.

Now think how much people should know the God who has made them. But they did not. Even when God came to visit them, to live among them, they did not recognise him.

They did not want to know him.

Study passage

We read here of how people deliberately refused to see who Jesus really was. Notice what the (police) officers sent by the Pharisees and chief priests to arrest Jesus, thought about him: 'No man ever spoke like this man'.

In spite of this the Pharisees and chief priests refused to believe in him.

The Pharisees and the chief priests sent officers to take him... Then the officers came to the chief priests and Pharisees, who said to them, 'Why have you not brought him?'

The officers answered, 'No man ever spoke like this man!' Then the Pharisees answered them, 'Are you also deceived? Have any of the rulers or the Pharisees believed in him? But this crowd that does not know the law is accursed.'

John 7, vv.32, 45–52

He came to his own, and his own did not receive him.

When Jesus came into the world, born in Bethlehem at the time of Caesar Augustus (around the year 4 A.D.), he came to his own people: the Jews.

Because Jesus is the eternal Word of God, he had been speaking to the Jews all through their history — from the time of Abraham to the time of Malachi.

So it often says in the Old Testament: 'the word of the Lord came to ...'; or 'thus says the Lord'; or 'the word of the Lord said...'

The Jews then should have recognised Jesus. But even they — God's own people — did not welcome him in. They treated him as an outsider.

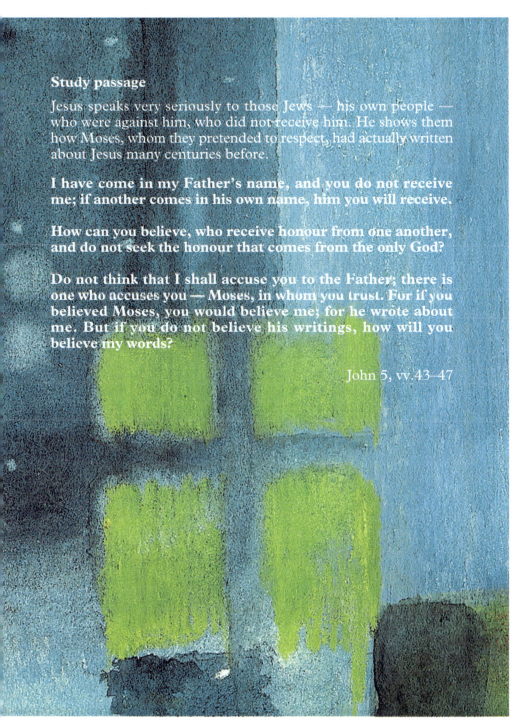

Study passage

Jesus speaks very seriously to those Jews — his own people —
who were against him, who did not receive him. He shows them
how Moses, whom they pretended to respect, had actually written
about Jesus many centuries before.

**I have come in my Father's name, and you do not receive
me; if another comes in his own name, him you will receive.**

**How can you believe, who receive honour from one another,
and do not seek the honour that comes from the only God?**

**Do not think that I shall accuse you to the Father; there is
one who accuses you — Moses, in whom you trust. For if you
believed Moses, you would believe me; for he wrote about
me. But if you do not believe his writings, how will you
believe my words?**

John 5, vv.43–47

But as many as received him, to them he gave the right to become children of God, even to those who believe in his name.

When someone knocks at your door, you ask: 'Who's that?' They answer: 'The plumber' or 'the electrician' (their title). Or they may say, 'It's me — Sally' (their name). If you recognise them, or know who they are, from their name or title, you let them in.

If you don't know the person who calls, you don't welcome them in — you don't receive them.

So it was when Jesus came to people. Some people received him — they let him in. Why was that? Because they believed in his name: they recognised him.

Jesus' name is his title: Jesus means Saviour. He said, 'I'm Jesus, the Saviour.' When people believed in Jesus' name, they believed he was the Saviour. That was letting him in.

To those people, Jesus gave the right to become the children of God.

Study passage

This is an example of a group of people who were not Jewish, but who came to believe in the name of Jesus. The fourth chapter of John's Gospel tells us about a Samaritan woman who received Jesus. She had told the people of her city how Jesus — a stranger — had known all about her life: 'he told me all that ever I did'. As a result they in turn came to hear Jesus, and to believe in his name: the Christ, the Saviour of the world.

And many of the Samaritans of the city believed in him because of the word of the woman who testified, 'he told me all that I ever did'.

So when the Samaritans had come to him, they urged him to stay with them; and he stayed there two days. And many more believed because of his own word.

Then they said to the woman, 'Now we believe, not because of what you said, for we have heard for ourselves and know that this is indeed the Christ, the Saviour of the world.'

John 4, vv.39–42

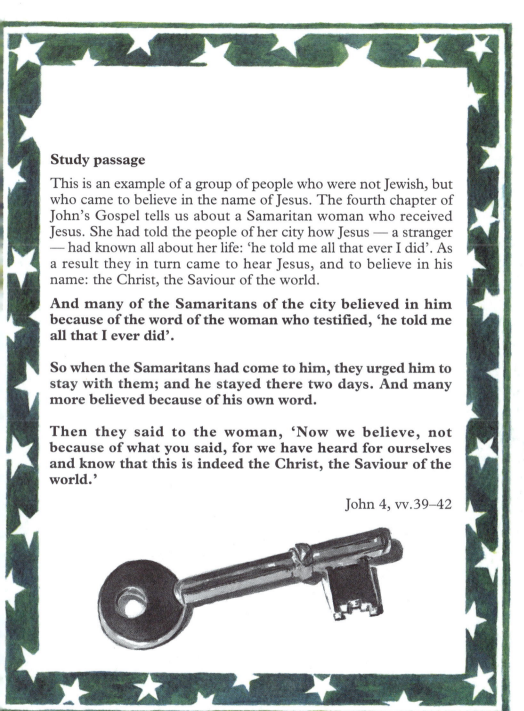

To them he gave the right to become the children of God

When you come home from school, you don't just walk into any house, thinking it will be your home. You go into the house which belongs to your family — that is your home. Children have the right to be in their own house.

When Adam and Eve were in the garden of Eden, they were God's children. The Garden was a home for them, the house of God where they were with their Father.

But when they sinned against God, they were shut out from the garden. They lost the right to be God's children. They could not stay at home with him.

But before he sent them away, God gave Adam and Eve a promised way back — like a key to their old home. God said: 'Believe in the Saviour I will send.'

When Jesus spoke to people he said: 'Believe in me — the Saviour.' Some people believed this: to them Jesus gave the right to become the children of God. This is the key which we must use.

Study passage

This is the beginning of the story of Lazarus, which we looked at earlier. Martha's brother, Lazarus, had just died. Martha had sent for Jesus some days before, but Jesus had only come to help when it seemed too late: Lazarus died before he arrived. But Jesus uses this death to help Martha understand that he is the person who gives everlasting life. Martha is able to believe in his name. To her, he gave the right to become one of the children of God.

Then Martha, as soon as she heard that Jesus was coming, went and met him... Then Martha said to Jesus, 'Lord, if you had been here, my brother would not have died. But even now I know that whatever you ask of God, God will give you.' Jesus said to her, 'Your brother will rise again.' Martha said to him, 'I know that he will rise again in the resurrection at the last day'. Jesus said to her, 'I am the resurrection and the life. He who believes in me, even though he dies, he shall live. And whoever lives and believes in me shall never die. Do you believe this?' She said to him, 'Yes, Lord, I believe that you are the Christ, the Son of God, who is to come into the world.'

John 11, vv.20–27

Who were born not of blood, nor of the will of the flesh, nor of the will of man, but of God.

A baby cannot decide to be born. It is born because that is what its father and mother wanted.

The people who believed in Jesus, and who were given the right to become God's children, were born of God. They were born into God's family, because that was what he wanted. It was not something which they decided: they could not decide to be born, any more than a baby can.

Only God could decide that they should be born into his family.

Study passage

The Pharisees were a group of religious Jews who were specially against Jesus. In this story one of them, Nicodemus, comes to Jesus at night time — probably so that no one should know that he had come. Jesus explains to him what it means to be born of God. Nicodemus is surprised that Jesus tells him that he cannot even *see* the kingdom of God until he is born again in this way.

Jesus said to him [Nicodemus], 'Most assuredly, I say to you, unless one is born again, he cannot see the kingdom of God'. Nicodemus said to him, 'How can a man be born when he is old? Can he enter a second time into his mother's womb and be born?' Jesus answered, 'Most assuredly, I say to you, unless one is born of water and the Spirit, he cannot enter the kingdom of God. That which is born of the flesh is flesh, and that which is born of the Spirit is spirit. Do not marvel that I said to you, 'You must be born again'. The wind blows where it wishes, and you hear the sound of it, but cannot tell where it comes from and where it goes. So is everyone who is born of the Spirit'.

John 3, vv.3–8

Born, not of blood...

John knew that people would think the opposite of what Jesus told Nicodemus.

They would think that being born into God's family is up to us — not up to God. Some people would think it was something that you inherited: that being born into God's family is handed down from parents to children — born 'of blood'. The Jews often thought that being a Jew was the key into God's house: if you were born a Jew you were born a son of God.

But John says none of this is true.

He says that the right to become the sons of God is given to those who are born of God. It is up to God — not up to us. It is God who brings us to birth into his family — by his Spirit, not 'of blood', — or family connection.

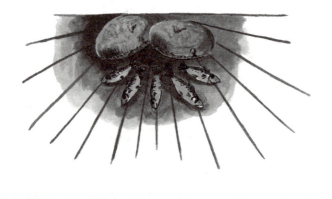

Study passage

Jesus says that without the work of God the Father no one can be saved. As he did so often, he gives a picture of himself, this time, as the bread of life coming down from heaven. Jesus had put this truth into an action picture, by feeding 5000 people with five loaves and two fishes. When he did this he showed that what he said about himself being the bread of life was really true. Only God could say and do these things.

The Jews then murmured against him, because he said, 'I am the bread which came down from heaven.' And they said, 'Is not this Jesus, the son of Joseph, whose father and mother we know? How is it then that he says, "I have come down from heaven"?'
Jesus therefore answered and said to them, 'Do not murmur among yourselves. No one can come to me unless the Father who sent me draws him; and I will raise him up at the last day. It is written in the prophets, "And they shall all be taught by God". Therefore everyone who has heard and learned from the Father comes to me. Not that anyone has seen the Father, except he who is from God, he has seen the Father.
Most assuredly, I say to you, he who believes in me has everlasting life. I am the bread of life.'

John 6, vv.41–48

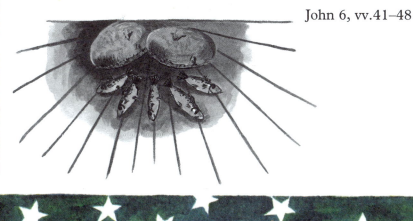

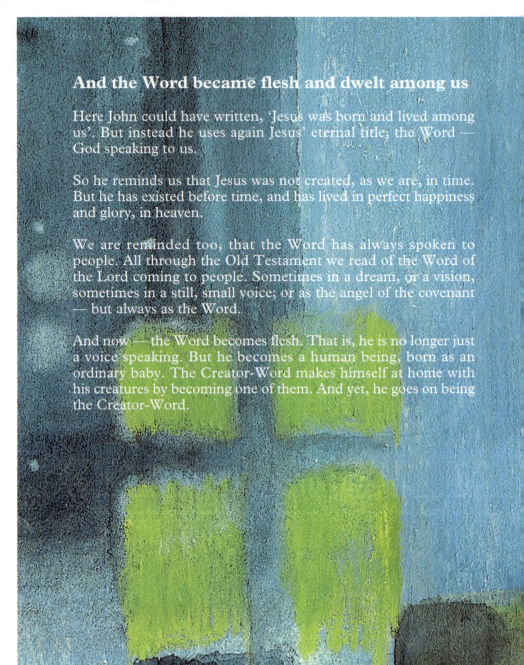

And the Word became flesh and dwelt among us

Here John could have written, 'Jesus was born and lived among us'. But instead he uses again Jesus' eternal title, the Word — God speaking to us.

So he reminds us that Jesus was not created, as we are, in time. But he has existed before time, and has lived in perfect happiness and glory, in heaven.

We are reminded too, that the Word has always spoken to people. All through the Old Testament we read of the Word of the Lord coming to people. Sometimes in a dream, or a vision, sometimes in a still, small voice; or as the angel of the covenant — but always as the Word.

And now — the Word becomes flesh. That is, he is no longer just a voice speaking. But he becomes a human being, born as an ordinary baby. The Creator-Word makes himself at home with his creatures by becoming one of them. And yet, he goes on being the Creator-Word.

Study passage

This is a hard part of John's Gospel to understand. Looking at Jesus, his listeners see just an ordinary man — flesh — living (or dwelling) among them.

But Jesus tells them he has come from above — from heaven — and that he is not of this world. He speaks of God the Father as 'he that sent me'. He is the Word, speaking to the world those things which he has heard from his Father.

But his listeners do not understand: they are of this world.

And he [Jesus] said to them, 'You are from beneath; I am from above. You are of this world; I am not of this world. Therefore I said to you that you will die in your sins; for if you do not believe that I am he, you will die in your sins.' Then they said to him, 'Who are you?'

And Jesus said to them, 'Just what I have been saying to you from the beginning. I have many things to say and to judge concerning you, but he who sent me is true; and I speak to the world those things which I heard from him.' They did not understand that he spoke to them of the Father.

John 8, vv.23–27

And we beheld his glory, the glory as of the only begotten of the Father

Imagine a rich prince coming from his palace to visit some very poor people in their houses. Perhaps he gets out of his beautiful car and comes to shake people's hands. Then he waves and leaves.

But now imagine the prince takes a case from his car and comes to live in those filthy houses. Soon the people feel he is one of them: he has made himself at home with them. Nothing of the glory of the palace is left for him — only dirt and poverty, hunger and disease.

But if someone who knew his father looked carefully, they would see that the prince was like his father, the king: that is his glory.

So it was with John, when he saw the Word made flesh, living among us. The glory Jesus had was not in what he looked like — he looked like a man, and men are sinful. (Jesus was not sinful, but he looked like men, who are). The glory Jesus had was in what he was — the only begotten of the Father, full of grace and truth.

Study passage

Jesus speaks to his disciples just before he left them in this world and went back to heaven — his Father's house.

We can see how slowly the disciples realised that Jesus was the only begotten of the Father, full of grace and truth. Jesus is perfectly like his Father. The person who has seen him has seen the Father. They are one God.

[Jesus talks about how he is going back to heaven]. **Thomas said to him, 'Lord, we do not know where you are going, and how can we know the way?'**

Jesus said to him, 'I am the way, the truth and the life. No one comes to the Father except through me. If you had known me, you would have known my Father also; and from now on you know him and have seen him.'

Philip said to him, 'Lord, show us the Father, and it is sufficient for us.'

Jesus said to him, 'Have I been with you so long, and yet you have not known me, Philip? He who has seen me has seen the Father; so how can you say, 'Show us the Father'? Do you not believe that I am in the Father, and the Father in me?'

John 14, vv.1-10

43

Full of grace and truth

What is God like? That is a question people often ask. In the Old Testament, long before John wrote his book, Moses had asked God to show him his glory. God did this by talking to him, and telling Moses what he was like:

'The Lord, the Lord God, merciful and gracious, long-suffering and abundant in goodness and truth.'*

Now, when John comes to describe Jesus, he makes a note of how he carefully watched the glory which Jesus had, and saw that it was the same glory — the glory of the only begotten of the Father — full of grace and truth. Or, 'abundant in goodness and truth'.*

God's glory is not in what he looks like, nor even in what he has made, but in what he is, and what he does. Moses was told about this. But John lived with God the Son and saw his glory every day.

*Exodus 34 v. 6

Study passage

Jesus speaks in prayer to his Father about the glory he has. He is just about to die on the cross — this was the work the Father had given him to do. He is full of grace: he is going to die in order to save his enemies. He is full of truth: he has devoted his life to speaking and showing the words the only true God has given him.

Jesus spoke these words, lifted up his eyes to heaven, and said: 'Father, the hour has come. Glorify your Son, that your Son also may glorify you, as you have given him authority over all flesh, that he should give eternal life to as many as you have given him. And this is eternal life, that they may know you, the only true God, and Jesus Christ whom you have sent.
I have glorified you on the earth. I have finished the work which you have given me to do. And now, O Father, glorify me together with yourself, with the glory which I had with you before the world was.
I have manifested your name to the men whom you have given me out of the world. They were yours, you gave them to me, and they have kept your word. Now they have known that all things which you have given me are from you. For I have given to them the words which you have given me; and they have received them, and have known surely that I came forth from you; and they have believed that you sent me.

John 17, vv.1–8

Full of grace

Imagine two people. One has a car. The other has a washing machine. But neither of them has paid for these things. They are both in debt to the shop owners, owing them large amounts of money.

When these two people meet, one asks the other: 'Give me some money please.' But he replies: 'I can't — I already owe a huge sum. I am in debt myself.'

Who can help these people? No one. Unless the shop owner comes and pays the debt himself.

That would almost be too good to be true!

This is a picture of people being in debt to God — not with money, but because of their sins.

Everyone is in debt to God, even people like Mary, Jesus' mother, or Peter, Jesus' disciple.

The Bible shows us that none of them was perfect: each one was born in sin, and had sins which needed paying for. So we cannot get grace, or forgiveness, from them. They also are in debt to God.

Who can help us then? No-one — unless God himself comes and offers to pay the debt which we owe him.

That is what John is speaking of when he says that Jesus is full of grace. Grace is a quality which only God has: it is the kindness which he shows to people who do not deserve it; the forgiveness which he gives freely to people who are in debt to him because of their sins. Jesus is full of this grace. He has no sins of his own, and he is God, who alone can forgive sin.

Study passage

Jesus, by a picture in action, shows how he washes away sin.

Notice how quickly Peter agrees to Jesus washing him, once he realises it is a sign of his being washed clean of his sins.

Jesus, by this sign, shows that he is full of grace.

Jesus... rose from supper and laid aside his garments, took a towel and girded himself. After that, he poured water into a basin and began to wash the disciples' feet, and to wipe them with the towel with which he was girded. Then he came to Simon Peter. And Peter said to him, 'Lord, are you washing my feet?' Jesus answered and said to him, 'What I am doing you do not understand now, but you will know after this.'

Peter said to him, 'You shall never wash my feet!' Jesus answered him, 'If I do not wash you, you have no part with me.' Simon Peter said to him, 'Lord, not my feet only, but also my hands and my head!'

John 13, vv.4–9

Full of truth

Think of your life as though it were a tower you can build out of blocks. Right from the beginning it is not upright. The more it is built up, the more it leans over, until it completely falls over. So our lives start off by not being true to God's standards. And the longer we live, the further away from God's truth we go — unless God's grace changes us.

But when the Word became flesh — when Jesus was born — his earthly life was prefectly right and true, from the beginning. It was completely true to God's standards: like a tower which is true and upright, perfectly reliable and trustworthy.

We cannot put our trust in any mere human being.

Our trust must be in God the Son.

Only he is truly trustworthy: only he is full of truth.

Study passage

Why was Jesus born? Why did he come into the world? Why did the Word become flesh? Jesus gives us the answer in this passage: it is to be a witness to the truth. All he says is truthful. He is full of truth. In this passage, John describes Jesus on trial before the Roman governor, Pontius Pilate.

Pilate asks the question, 'What is truth?', but he does not really want to know the answer. That is how people deliberately push God's truth further and further away from themselves. Jesus said of himself, 'I am the truth.' Here, Pilate sends him to be scourged and then crucified.

Pilate therefore said to him, 'Are you a king then?'
Jesus answered, 'You say rightly that I am a king. For this cause I was born, and for this cause I have come into the world, that I should bear witness to the truth. Everyone who is of the truth hears my voice.'

Pilate said to him, 'What is truth?' And when he had said this, he went out again to the Jews, and said to them, 'I find no fault in him at all. But you have a custom that I should release someone to you at the Passover. Do you therefore want me to release to you the King of the Jews?'

Then they all cried again, saying, 'Not this man, but Barabbas!' Now Barabbas was a robber. So then Pilate took Jesus and scourged him.

John 18, vv.37–40. John 19, v.1

John bore witness of him

All through Old Testament times the Word of God had spoken to the people of Israel. The last prophet who spoke God's Word was called Malachi. After him, there were no other prophets for 400 years.

It seemed as though God had stopped speaking to his people.

But then, John the Baptist was sent by God.

Everyone in Israel realised that here again was a prophet, speaking the Word of the Lord. Imagine how important he must have seemed. Even the religious leaders went to hear what he said.

Study passage

Jesus speaks here to the Jews about the witness of John. A witness is someone who sees something and who gives evidence of what he sees to other people. John saw Jesus, and witnessed that he was the person whom God was sending as the Saviour. But Jesus adds that the miracles (which he calls 'the works') that he does are an even greater witness than John. They showed even more clearly that he was the person whom God was sending as the Saviour.

[Jesus said] **'If I bear witness of myself, my witness is not true. There is another who bears witness of me, and I know that the witness which he witnesses of me is true. You sent to John, and he has borne witness to the truth. Yet I do not receive testimony from man, but I say these things that you may be saved. He was the burning and shining lamp, and you were willing for a time to rejoice in his light. But I have a greater witness than John's; for the works which the Father has given me to finish — the very works that I do bear witness of me, that the Father has sent me.'**

John 5, vv. 31–36

John cried out saying, 'This was he of whom I said, "He who comes after me is preferred before me, for he was before me" '.

John the Baptist's words are almost like a riddle. He talks about Jesus as the one who comes after him. This was because John's great work was to get things ready for Jesus — who was coming after him.

But to people at the time John himself seemed so important — the first prophet after such a long time. So John tells them that although he comes first in time, the one who comes second is in fact more important.

Jesus comes second, but he overtakes John. Why is that?

'Because', says John, 'he was before me!' Jesus is the eternal Word, who has been speaking all through Old Testament times.

He is the everlasting preacher, the great Prophet: he is the living Word of God.

Study passge

God spoke to Malachi, the last Old Testament prophet, about John the Baptist: 'Behold, I send my messenger, and he will prepare the way before me.'

Then he spoke about Jesus: 'And the Lord, whom you seek, will suddenly come to his temple, even the Messenger of the covenant...'

Now we read of how Jesus actually comes to the temple — his temple — his Father's house — and sends packing all the people who had turned it into a rowdy shopping centre.

Now the Passover of the Jews was at hand, and Jesus went up to Jerusalem. And he found in the temple those who sold oxen and sheep and doves, and the money-changers doing business. When he had made a whip of cords, he drove them all out of the temple, with the sheep and the oxen, and poured out the coins of the money-changers and overturned the tables.
And he said to those who sold doves, 'Take these things away! Do not make my Father's house a house of merchandise!' Then his disciples remembered that it was written, 'Zeal for your house has eaten me up'.

John 2, vv.13–17

And of his fullness we have all received

A tree may be full of beautiful fruit. But perhaps those particular fruit only look lovely — they cannot be eaten, because they are poisonous.

Or perhaps the tree belongs to someone else, and so we may not eat the fruit on it. It is good to see a tree full of fruit which we may eat — as many as we like: the tree is full.

John says that Jesus has a fullness. What does he mean? He is speaking about the fullness which belongs only to God. Everything human runs out: we never have enough love, enough patience, enough goodness. But the goodness and patience of God is never ending.

God is full of grace and truth.

Here John tells us that all believers in Jesus have received this fullness. It is something which is given to them freely.

Jesus is full of the fullness of God, and he gives this to his people.

Study passage

Jesus, using the picture of a vine, teaches how his people are joined to him — and so they receive his fullness.

The fruit they produce is their lives becoming more like Jesus: full of grace and truth.

If they are not joined to him, they cannot produce this fruit.

I am the true vine, and my Father is the vine-dresser. Every branch in me that does not bear fruit he takes away; and every branch that bears fruit he prunes, that it may bear more fruit. You are already clean because of the word which I have spoken to you.

Abide [stay] in me, and I in you. As the branch cannot bear fruit of itself, unless it abides in the vine, neither can you, unless you abide in me.

I am the vine, you are the branches. He who abides in me, and I in him, bears much fruit; for without me you can do nothing. If anyone does not abide in me, he is cast out as a branch and is withered; and they gather them and throw them into the fire and they are burned.

John 15, vv.1–6

And grace for grace

When you turn on the windscreen wiper in a car it wipes away the rain on the car window all the time.

As soon as the window is blurred, the wiper clears away the rain drops, time and time again.

All the time a Christian is alive, he goes on sinning against God. And all the time, the grace of God wipes the sin away time and time again.

Jesus is full of grace — it is never ending. And he never stops showing grace to his people: grace for grace.

56

Study passage

One day Jesus spoke to a Samaritan woman. At first he asks her for a drink. Then he goes on to tell her about 'living water' — a picture of the never-ending grace of God which *he* will give *her*. The woman doesn't understand what he means — she doesn't realise he is using picture language. Then Jesus explains what he means by 'living water': God's grace which goes on and on for ever.

Jesus answered and said to her [the Samaritan woman]: 'If you knew the gift of God, and who it is who says to you, "Give me a drink", you would have asked him, and he would have given you living water.'
The woman said to him, 'Sir, you have nothing to draw with, and the well is deep. Where then do you get that living water?... Jesus answered and said to her, 'Whoever drinks of this water will thirst again, but whoever drinks of the water that I shall give him will never thirst. But the water that I shall give him will become in him a fountain of water springing up into everlasting life.'

John 4, vv.11–14

For the law was given through Moses

God's law was given to Moses, and he gave it to the people of Israel.

The law of God teaches two great things: what God is like, and what he expects us to be like. It was summed up in the ten commandments.

Even as Moses carried the two tablets of stone (with the ten commandments written on them) down the mountain to the people, the people were breaking those commandments. Then Moses himself threw down the stones and broke them.

The law of God, given to Moses, was always — from the beginning — to show people that they are law-breakers. They need God's forgiveness. This was the next great lesson, which the law given by Moses taught.

Study passage

Jesus here makes it quite plain that no-one can keep the law of God which was given through Moses.

Only he himself has no unrighteousness: only he seeks the glory of the one who sent him — the glory of God. Jesus alone keeps the law of God, and yet the Jews were trying to kill him.

Now about the middle of the feast, Jesus went up into the temple and taught.

And the Jews marvelled, saying, 'How does this man know letters, never having studied?'

Jesus answered and said, 'My doctrine is not mine, but his who sent me. If anyone wants to do his will, he shall know concerning the doctrine, whether it is from God or whether I speak on my own authority. He who speaks from himself seeks his own glory; but he who seeks the glory of the one who sent him is true, and no unrighteousness is in him.

Did not Moses give you the law, and yet none of you keeps the law? Why do you seek to kill me?'

John 7, vv.14–19

But grace and truth came through Jesus Christ

The forgiveness of God — God's grace — comes by Jesus Christ. It is for law-breakers: for people who have broken the commandments. And it is given to them by Jesus Christ — grace for grace, from his fullness.

No mere man, not even Moses, could give forgiveness.

Only God can forgive those who break his law. It is his free gift, and he gives it to sinners who do not deserve it.

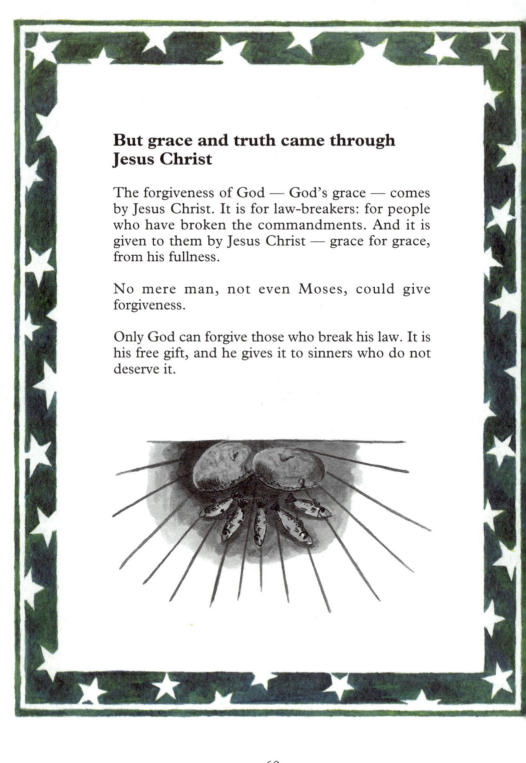

Study passage

Jesus talks about the salvation he gives to sinners. He has just fed 5,000 people with five loaves and two fish. This is a sign that he is able to feed people with salvation. He startles his listeners with the picture he uses. People will die if they do not have food — bread. People will die if they do not have the bread of life — Jesus. But Jesus himself is going to die. He is going to give his life, his 'flesh' for the life of the world.

So in this way people must eat the bread of his 'flesh': they must believe that his death — the giving of his life — is the only way that they can have life from heaven — the only way that they can bc saved from death.

[Jesus said:] **'Most assuredly, I say to you, he who believes in me has everlasting life.**
I am the bread of life.
Your fathers ate the manna in the wilderness, and are dead. This is the bread which came down from heaven. If anyone eats of this bread, he will live for ever; and the bread that I shall give is my flesh, which I shall give for the life of the world.'

John 6, vv.47–51

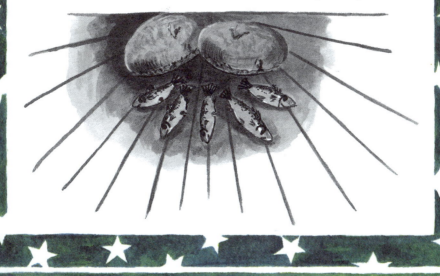

Truth came through Jesus Christ

There are some mirrors which are made so that when we look in them they distort our image: we look very thin and tall, or very round and short.

When God made the first man, Adam, he made him to be like himself — in his own image — perfectly upright. When Adam sinned against God, this distorted the image of God, so that mankind was no longer like God, but twisted and distorted like Satan, God's enemy.

Satan is the father of lies. Everything he says about God is false and crooked. All through time he has been pointing to the twisted image of man, and saying that God is like that too. People always picture God as being like themselves, only bigger. That lie came from Satan.

When Jesus came into the world, he truly was like God — he was perfectly upright. Unlike Adam, he never sinned: he kept all the commandments. And so the image of God was kept perfect. Everything he said about God was true. He could point to himself as the true image of God, and say that God is like that. We must not picture God as being like ourselves: he is not. That is a lie from Satan. We must know that God is like his Son. The truth (about God) came through Jesus Christ.

Study passage

Jesus talks very strongly about Satan and his lies. And about his own work of telling the truth.

Jesus said to them, 'If God were your Father, you would love me, for I proceeded forth and came from God; nor have I come of myself, but he sent me.

Why do you not understand my speech? Because you are not able to listen to my word. You are of your father the devil, and the desires of your father you want to do. He was a murderer from the beginning, and does not stand in the truth, because there is no truth in him. When he speaks a lie, he speaks from his own resources, for he is a liar and the father of it.

But because I tell the truth, you do not believe me. Which of you convicts me of sin? And if I tell the truth, why do you not believe me?

He who is of God hears God's word; therefore you do not hear, because you are not of God.

John 8, vv.42–47

No one has seen God at any time

When we have a difficult problem we sometimes say, 'I just can't see that'. Or, when we have understood, we say, 'I can see now'.

Here John uses the word 'see' in the same way. No one has seen — or perfectly understood about — God, at any time.

God is invisible. He is a Spirit, and has no body. So in this way also we cannot see God.

But it is not that sort of seeing that John is mainly talking about here. It is the 'seeing' of our understanding.

Study passage

John tells us that ordinary people, who are just 'earthly', can only talk about things which happen here, on earth. None of them has seen God at any time, so they cannot talk about heavenly things. Jesus is not an ordinary person: he has come to earth from heaven, and so he can tell us about God.

'He who comes from above is above all; he who is of the earth is earthly and speaks of the earth. He who comes from heaven is above all.

And what he has seen and heard, that he testifies; and no one receives his testimony. He who has received his testimony has certified that God is true.

For he whom God has sent speaks the words of God, for God does not give the Spirit by measure. The Father loves the Son, and has given all things into his hand.

He who believes in the Son has everlasting life; and he who does not believe the Son shall not see life, but the wrath of God abides on him.'

John 3, vv.31–36

The only begotten Son, who is in the bosom of the Father, he has declared him

Imagine someone goes to a school, and asks about a particular teacher. He asks one of the children: 'Do you know Mr Brown?' The child explains what the teacher looks like, and a few things he knows about him. But supposing the same person speaks to the teacher's son: 'Do you know Mr Brown?' How much more he would be able to say about his own father!

In the Old Testament we are told that Moses knew some things about God. God showed him a part of his glory when he declared, 'The Lord, the Lord God, merciful and gracious, long-suffering, and abundant in goodness and truth'.*

But in this way, Moses was like the first child in the school: he only knew what God chose to show him.

John describes Jesus as the only begotten Son. He is completely different from any one else. He is God's only Son, who is close to his Father in a way that no-one else can be. He sees God — he perfectly understands him — and he declares, or tells us, what God is really like.

* Exodus 34, v.6

Study passage

This passage tells us more about how Jesus and his Father are completely at one. It helps us to understand better what John means when he says that Jesus is 'in the bosom of the Father'.

Then Jesus ... said ... 'Most assuredly, I say to you, the Son can do nothing of himself, but what he sees the Father do; for whatever he does, the Son also does in like manner. For the Father loves the Son, and shows him all things that he himself does; and he will show him greater works than these, that you may marvel.

For as the Father raises the dead and gives life to them, even so the Son gives life to whom he will. For the Father judges no one, but has committed all judgment to the Son, that all should honour the Son just as they honour the Father. He who does not honour the Son does not honour the Father who sent him.'

John 5, vv.19–23

67